CW00419836

by Iain Gray

Lang**Syne**

PUBLISHING

WRITING *to* REMEMBER

Lang**Syne**

PUBLISHING

WRITING *to* REMEMBER

79 Main Street, Newtongrange,
Midlothian EH22 4NA
Tel: 0131 344 0414   Fax: 0845 075 6085
E-mail: info@lang-syne.co.uk
www.langsyneshop.co.uk

Design by Dorothy Meikle
Printed by Printwell Ltd
© Lang Syne Publishers Ltd 2019

ISBN 978-1-85217-208-4

Russell

MOTTO:

What Will Be Will Be.

*Echoes of a far distant past
can still be found in most names*

Chapter one:

Origins of Scottish surnames

by George Forbes

It all began with the Normans.

For it was they who introduced surnames into common usage more than a thousand years ago, initially based on the title of their estates, local villages and chateaux in France to distinguish and identify these landholdings, usually acquired at the point of a bloodstained sword.

Such grand descriptions also helped enhance the prestige of these arrogant warlords and generally glorify their lofty positions high above the humble serfs slaving away below in the pecking order who only had single names, often with Biblical connotations as in Pierre and Jacques.

The only descriptive distinctions among this peasantry concerned their occupations, like Pierre the swineherd or Jacques the ferryman.

The Normans themselves were originally Vikings (or Northmen) who raided, colonised and eventually settled down around the French coastline.

They had sailed up the Seine in their longboats in 900AD under their ferocious leader Rollo and ruled the roost in north east France before sailing over to conquer England, bringing their relatively new tradition of having surnames with them.

It took another hundred years for the Normans to percolate northwards and surnames did not begin to appear in Scotland until the thirteenth century.

These adventurous knights brought an aura of chivalry with them and it was said no damsel of any distinction would marry a man unless he had at least two names.

The family names included that of Scotland's great hero Robert De Brus and his compatriots were warriors from families like the De Morevils, De Umphravils, De Berkelais, De Quincis, De Viponts and De Vaux.

As the knights settled the boundaries of their vast estates, they took territorial names, as in Hamilton, Moray, Crawford, Cunningham, Dunbar, Ross, Wemyss, Dundas, Galloway, Renfrew, Greenhill, Hazelwood, Sandylands and Church-hill.

Other names, though not with any obvious geographical or topographical features, nevertheless derived from ancient parishes like Douglas, Forbes, Dalyell and Guthrie.

Other surnames were coined in connection with occupations, castles or legendary deeds.

Stuart originated in the word steward, a prestigious post which was an integral part of any large medieval household. The same applied to Cooks, Chamberlains, Constables and Porters.

Borders towns and forts – needed in areas like the Debateable Lands which were constantly fought over by feuding local families – had their own distinctive names; and it was often from them that the resident groups took their communal titles, as in the Grahams of Annandale, the Elliots and Armstrongs of the East Marches, the Scotts and Kerrs of Teviotdale and Eskdale.

Even physical attributes crept into surnames, as in Small, Little and More (the latter being 'beg' in Gaelic), Long or Lang, Stark, Stout, Strong or Strang and even Jolly.

Mieklejohns would have had the strength of several men, while Littlejohn was named after the legendary sidekick of Robin Hood.

Colours got into the act with Black, White, Grey, Brown and Green (Red developed into Reid, Ruddy or Ruddiman). Blue was rare and nobody ever wanted to be associated with yellow.

Pompous worthies took the name Wiseman, Goodman and Goodall.

Words intimating the sons of leading figures were soon affiliated into the language as in Johnson, Adamson, Richardson and Thomson, while the Norman equivalent of Fitz (from the French-Latin 'filius' meaning 'son') cropped up in Fitzmaurice and Fitzgerald.

The prefix 'Mac' was 'son of' in Gaelic and clans often originated with occupations – as in

MacNab being sons of the Abbot, MacPherson and MacVicar being sons of the minister and MacIntosh being sons of the chief.

The church's influence could be found in the names Kirk, Clerk, Clarke, Bishop, Friar and Monk. Proctor came from a church official, Singer and Sangster from choristers, Gilchrist and Gillies from Christ's servant, Mitchell, Gilmory and Gilmour from servants of St Michael and Mary, Malcolm from a servant of Columba and Gillespie from a bishop's servant.

The rudimentary medical profession was represented by Barber (a trade which also once included dentistry and surgery) as well as Leech or Leitch.

Businessmen produced Merchants, Mercers, Monypennies, Chapmans, Sellers and Scales, while down at the old village watermill the names that cropped up included Miller, Walker and Fuller.

Other self explanatory trades included Coopers, Brands, Barkers, Tanners, Skinners, Brewsters and Brewers, Tailors, Saddlers, Wrights,

Cartwrights, Smiths, Harpers, Joiners, Sawyers, Masons and Plumbers.

Even the scenery was utilised as in Craig, Moor, Hill, Glen, Wood and Forrest.

Rank, whether high or low, took its place with Laird, Barron, Knight, Tennant, Farmer, Husband, Granger, Grieve, Shepherd, Shearer and Fletcher.

The hunt and the chase supplied Hunter, Falconer, Fowler, Fox, Forrester, Archer and Spearman.

The renowned medieval historian Froissart, who eulogised about the romantic deeds of chivalry (and who condemned Scotland as being a poverty stricken wasteland), once sniffily dismissed the peasantry of his native France as the jacquerie (or the jacques-without-names) but it was these same humble folk who ended up overthrowing the arrogant aristocracy.

In the olden days, only the blueblooded knights of antiquity were entitled to full, proper names, both Christian and surnames, but with the passing of time and a more egalitarian, less feudal atmosphere, more respectful and worthy titles spread throughout the populace as a whole.

Echoes of a far distant past can still be found in most names and they can be borne with pride in commemoration of past generations who fought and toiled in some capacity or other to make our nation what it now is, for good or ill.

Chapter two:

In freedom's cause

**In England it is the family name of the
Dukes of Bedford, while in Scotland generations of Russells have also achieved fame
and honours.**

It is one of the earliest recorded surnames
in Scotland, with a Walter Russell recorded as
having witnessed a charter in Paisley, in the west,
at some stage between 1164 and 1177 and a
Robert Russell recorded in the east between 1180
and 1220.

That the name should be on record at such
early dates should perhaps come as no surprise
when we learn that it was originally a descriptive
name, stemming from 'rous' or 'rousel', meaning
'red': the name would have originally applied to
someone with red hair, of which there have
always been many in Scotland!

Variations of the name have included
Russel, Russall, Rusel, and Russale and, in

common with other names that were originally descriptive, Russell gradually became a surname proper, and was to be found all over Scotland.

The signature of a Robert Russell of Berwickshire, for example, is to be found on the humiliating treaty of fealty to the conquering Edward I, Hammer of the Scots, in 1296.

Signed by 1,500 earls, bishops, and burgesses such as Russell, the parchment is known as the *Ragman Roll* because of the profusion of ribbons that dangle from the seals of the signatories.

Rather ironically, the name was also 'imported' afresh to Scotland in 1333 in the guise of an English baron who fought against the Scots at the side of Edward III at the siege of Berwick and the battle of Halidon Hill: a battle that marked a turning point not only in Scotland's history in general, but the fortunes of the Russells in particular.

The great warrior king Robert the Bruce had died in 1329 and was succeeded by the five-year-old David II.

Eager to take advantage of a dispute among the Scottish nobles over the young king's succession, an ambitious Edward gave his support to the rival Edward Balliol, confident he could use him as a mere puppet for his own imperialist aims.

A mighty English force invaded Scotland in August of 1332, defeating the Scots in battle at Dupplin Moor, near Perth. Balliol was enthroned as King of Scots at Scone the following month and, as Edward had plotted, swore fealty to him.

Nationalist passions were aroused, however, and Andrew Murray, who had been appointed Guardian of Scotland, raised the banner of revolt against the puppet Scots king and sent him fleeing across the border to his English master, Edward.

But in May of 1333 Edward returned with another army, including the English baron of the name of Russell, laid siege to Berwick Castle and met the Scots in battle at Halidon Hill, to the northwest of Berwick, on July 19.

Murray had already been captured and the

new Guardian was Archibald, Lord of Douglas, who arranged his forces in three tightly packed groups of spearmen known as schiltrons and a division of 1,200 knights.

They proved no match, however, for the deadly skill of the English archers and the knights who had taken better strategic advantage of the terrain.

The English victory was so complete that while Douglas, the earls of Ross, Sutherland and Carrick, 500 knights, seventy barons, and thousands of Scots foot soldiers were slain, the English were reported to have lost only fourteen men.

As a reward for his services in battle, a grateful and victorious Edward granted the Russell baron lands in Aberdeenshire, where he settled. Succeeding generations also acquired lands and became so powerful that they were granted heraldic arms and the descendants of the original English invader officially designated Russell of that Ilk.

Further lands were bought at the turn of

the seventeenth century near Elgin, followed later
by lands at Moncoffer, in Banffshire, and the
lands of Aden in Aberdeenshire.

Despite their own proud pedigree, the
Russells are also recognised by some authorities
as a sept of the equally proud Clan Cumming,
because they were territorial neighbours: this is
why the Russells are entitled to share in the clan's
heritage and traditions and why it is appropriate
for them to wear the Clan Cumming tartan.

It should also be stressed, however, that
it is probable that the Russell connection with
the Cummings pre-dates their settlement in the
northeast following the battle of Halidon Hill in
1333, because a 'native' community of Russells
may have already been settled there for several
centuries.

As kinsfolk of the Cummings, the Russells
would have shared in both the glorious fortunes
and tragic misfortunes of this clan whose crest is
a rampant lion wielding a sword and whose motto
is 'Courage'.

In common with what would become

many of Scotland's noble families, such as the Bruces and the Sinclairs, the Cummings, or Comyns, trace a pedigree back to those Normans who settled in England, and later in Scotland, in the wake of the invasion by William, Duke of Normandy in 1066.

The name is believed to derive from the town of Comines, in northern France, but some sources assert it may stem from the herb, 'cummin'.

The Cummings/Comyns owed their noble status to a Wilhelmus Comyn, Bishop of Durham, who was appointed Chancellor of Scotland in 1124 by David II, after moving north.

The Cummings/Comyns are most famously associated in Scottish history as being among the claimants to the throne, along with the Bruces, following the death of Alexander III in 1286.

There was never any love lost between the proud Comyns and the equally proud Bruces, and it was John Comyn of Badenoch, known to posterity as the Red Comyn, who was slain by the

then future king, Robert the Bruce, in the church
of the Greyfriars, in Dumfries, in 1306.

Comyn's role in the great struggle for
Scotland's freedom in the Wars of Independence
with England tends to be overshadowed by the

Robert the Bruce, King of Scots — *The Victor of Bannockburn*

undoubtedly glorious exploits of Bruce, and one of the almost forgotten facts of Scottish history is the decisive role Comyn played in defeating an English invasion force at the battle of Roslin, in present day Midlothian, in late February of 1303.

Robert Bruce had, albeit temporarily, 'come into the peace' of England's Edward I at the time, leaving Comyn as sole Guardian of Scotland, and it was in this capacity that he and Sir Simon Fraser led an 8,000 force of Scots to victory over a much numerically superior English force commanded by Sir John Segrave.

Included in Comyn's ranks would have been his own clansmen and kinsmen such as the Russells.

Few of the thousands of tourists who now flock annually to the mysterious Rosslyn Chapel, built more than 140 years after the battle and made particularly famous in recent years through the success of the American author Dan Brown's novel *The Da Vinci Code*, are aware that it stands on the site of where the Scots army were fed and had their wounds tended.

Chapter three:

Heretics and heroes

The tumultuous sixteenth, seventeenth, and early eighteenth centuries again see the Russells at the heart of Scotland's most bitter and bloody affairs.

These were centuries when Scotland experienced and had to suffer the dire consequences of civil wars caused by the struggles between Crown and Covenant and attempts to restore the exiled Royal House of Stuart to the throne.

Jerome Russell, a monk who was attached to the order of the Blackfriars in the diocese of the Archbishop of Glasgow, suffered the brutal fate of being burned at the stake as a heretic in 1539, along with 18-year-old Alexander Kennedy from Ayrshire and, more than 140 years later, another Russell would be at the centre of a murderous affair that sent shockwaves throughout the nation.

It had been on February 28, 1638, that the

historic National Covenant was first signed in the kirkyard of Greyfriars Church, in Edinburgh, with thousands of other ordinary folk subscribing to it as copies were circulated throughout the length and breadth of Scotland.

Those who adhered to the Covenant were known as Covenanters, who pledged to uphold the Presbyterian faith in defiance of the king's claim of supremacy in matters of religion, and many of them who were hounded by the merciless authorities literally took to the hills in the years following the signing of the Covenant to worship at what were known as open-air conventicles.

One of the sparks that lit the fuse of a subsequent armed rising by the Covenanters and what has become known to posterity as The Killing Time, came in May of 1679 when Archbishop James Sharp, the figurehead of what was known as Episcopalian authority in Scotland, was murdered on the moorland of Magus Moor as he made his way back from Edinburgh to St. Andrews.

The archbishop had been travelling along with his daughter, Isabel, and five servants when they were attacked by an armed band that had originally been lying in wait to ambush the Sheriff of Fife.

Realising Archbishop Sharp represented a much more attractive target, they dragged him from his coach and brutally stabbed him to death, despite his pleas for mercy.

The leader of the band of murderers, who appear to have firmly believed that the hapless archbishop actually represented the Anti-Christ, was the Covenanting John Balfour of Kinloch, and one of his compatriots was a James Russell.

A small bee is said to have flown from the archbishop's tobacco box while the murderers were rifling his belongings: this, it was believed, was actually his 'familiar', proving that he had been in league with the devil.

Both Balfour, Russell and other members of the band who had a hand in Sharp's murder became Covenanting heroes for their bloody deed, and Russell, in defence of their actions, later said Sharp 'had betrayed the Church as Judas, and had wrung his hands these eighteen or nineteen years in the blood of the saints.'

Only two of the murderers were ever captured and punished for Sharp's murder, but the wily Russell was not among them.

A celebrated Russell also figures in a conflict of a different kind, that of the internecine warfare that existed for centuries between the lawless clans and families that occupied both sides of the border.

The Treaty of York had been signed by Scotland's Alexander II in 1237, establishing the border with England as a line running from the Solway to the Tweed, but until as late as the seventeenth century the Borders became a byword for lawlessness.

There were three Marches, or areas of administration, on either side of the border – the West, Middle, and East Marches – all governed by a warden.

On the Scottish side of the border, the East March was dominated by the Homes and

Swintons, with the Kerrs, Douglases, and Elliots holding sway in the Middle March, and the Armstrongs, Maxwells and Johnstones in control of the West March.

Complaints from either side of the border, and there were many, were dealt with on Truce Days, with the wardens of the respective marches acting as arbitrators, while under a special law known as the Hot Trod, anyone who had their livestock stolen had the right to pursue the thieves and regain their property at the point of the sword.

In many cases, however, the wardens of the marches were far from arbitrary in their rulings, with self-interest governing their decisions, and as a result the Borders remained a scene of virtual anarchy, with no respect for either the English or the Scottish royal authority.

In July of 1575 Sir Francis Russell, a warden for one of the English Marches, attended a warden's court in what was known as the Debateable Land between the two borders, at Redeswire.

A dispute between the two sides arose and, in what became known as the Raid of the Redeswire, twenty-five of Sir Francis's men were killed and he himself taken prisoner for a time.

An indication of the lawlessness that prevailed in the wild and rugged borderland, despite the best efforts of the authorities on both sides to curb it, is that Sir Francis was killed a few years later in yet another border dispute.

In the Jacobite Risings of both 1715 and 1745, a state of virtual civil war existed in Scotland as even members of the same families took opposing sides: some supported the struggle to restore the exiled Royal House of Stuart to the throne, while others were firm in their support of the newly established Hanoverian monarchy.

The muster roll for the Jacobite army that was raised to fight for the cause of Prince Charles Edward Stuart, known as the Young Pretender, and who arrived on Scottish shores on August 19, 1745, includes a number of Russells.

It was on April 16, 1746, on Drummossie

Moor, near Inverness, that the decisive battle of
Culloden was fought, effectively sounding the
final death knell of not only the Jacobite cause,
but, in the brutal suppression that followed the
defeat, a way of life that had endured for
centuries.

    Included in the Jacobite muster roll is
Alexander Russell, from Edinburgh, who was
with the Duke of Perth's Regiment and was taken
prisoner at Carlisle.

    John Russell, a 24-year-old sail maker,
served with the Forfarshire (Ogilvy's Regiment)
and was wounded at Culloden, while 20-year-old

David Russell, a glove maker from Aberdeen, is recorded as having deserted from Lord Lewis Gordon's Regiment, then joining Stoneywood's Aberdeen Regiment before being taken prisoner after Culloden and transported to penal servitude in the colonies.

A noted family of Russells who appear to have been settled for centuries in the Scottish Borders gained honours for their military service in India on behalf of the mighty British Empire.

Known as the Russells of Ashiesteel, from near Selkirk, one of their most famous sons was Colonel William Russell who, as adjutant general of the Army of Madras, served under General Clive in his Indian campaigns between the mid-1750s to the mid-1760s.

His son, Major General Sir James Russell, also gained military honours as commander of a brigade of cavalry that fought with distinction at the battle of Mahedpoor in 1830.

Chapter four:

On the world stage

**Generations of Russells have achieved fame
and distinction in a number of other rather
more peaceful pursuits, ranging from political
reform and medical research to journalism,
philosophy and the stage.**

As an advisor to both England's Henry
VIII and Edward VI, John Russell was rewarded
with the title of Earl of Bedford in 1551, while
William Russell, the fifth earl, was created 1st
Duke of Bedford following the accession to the
throne of William of Orange in 1688.

Succeeding generations of the family
have gained international distinction, not least the
philosopher, mathematician and writer Bertrand
Russell, who was the 3rd Lord Russell.

Born in 1872, his paternal grandfather
was John Russell, the 1st Earl Russell, who
played a leading role in 1832 in securing British
parliamentary reform.

Bertrand Russell had a rather unconventional early life, apparently often contemplating suicide: he confided in his autobiography that it was only his interests in sex, religion and mathematics that kept him from this!

Imprisoned for a time during the First World War because of his pacifist activities, Russell was in later years a campaigner for nuclear disarmament and a critic of America's war in Vietnam.

He was made a Nobel Laureate in Literature in 1950, twenty years before his death in 1970 at the grand old age of 98.

One of his sons was Conrad Russell, the 5th Earl Russell who, before his death in 2004, had become recognised as a distinguished historian and politician.

The Edinburgh-born brothers Alexander and Patrick Russell, born in 1715 and 1727 respectively, gained distinction in the field of medical research.

Alexander contributed several papers to both the Royal Society and the Medical Society, while Patrick was responsible for an important study of plague.

In America, William Hepburn Russell, born in 1812, was the founder of the famed Pony Express, while in the world of journalism William Howard Russell, born in 1820, was the reporter for *The Times of London* who is recognised as one of the first war correspondents.

It was Russell who coined the phrase 'the thin red line' to describe the Highland infantry at the battle of Balaclava, during the Crimean War of 1854-56.

On the stage, Ernestine Jane Geraldine Russell is better known as the Hollywood actress Jane Russell, who was born in Minnesota in 1921 and is best known for her roles in films such as *The Outlaw* and *Gentlemen Prefer Blondes*.

Ken Russell, born in 1927, was the controversial British film director whose screen credits include *Women in Love*, *The Devils*, and *Valentino*. He died in 2011.

A rather less controversial but equally talented figure is William Martin Russell, the

British playwright, lyricist and composer born in 1947 whose play *Educating Rita* was filmed starring Michael Caine and Julie Walters.

There is also a renowned Russell of the four-legged variety – none other than the Jack Russell terrier, named after 'the sporting parson' John Russell who was responsible for developing the breed and who was a founder of Britain's prestigious Kennel Club!